The Town That Tried to Own Me

A Survival Story in Stages

"Survival was only the beginning."

by Flora Martin

Dedication

For the ones who survived the breaking,
and for the ones still piecing themselves back together.

For the ones who learned how to live on scraps,
but never forgot the taste of something more.

For the ones who stayed too long,
who loved too hard,
who forgave too often,
because they didn't know they were already enough.

For the ones who carried hope like a secret,
and dared to dream again after everything tried to silence them.

This is for you.
This is for every version of you.
This is proof that survival is only the beginning —
and you are allowed to want more.

You always were.

Note to the Reader

This book is stitched together from the quiet places —
the ones where the hurting lived, and the healing began.

I didn't write this to teach anyone how to survive.
I wrote this because sometimes, survival is too heavy to carry alone.

If you find pieces of yourself in these pages,
know that you are not broken.
You are not too late.
You are not too much.

You are the proof that surviving was never the end of your story.

Welcome home.

Table of Contents

Dedication

Note to the Reader

Table of Contents

Introduction

Breathing Because I Had To (*Silent Survival*)

The Lie I Lived (*Disillusionment*)

The Girl I Forgot (*Grieving the Old Self*)

Living on Leftovers (*Bittersweet Survival*)

I Was Never Theirs (*Defiance and Reclaiming*)

You Did What You Had To (*Compassion for the Past Self*)

Learning to Want Again (*Dreaming Again*)

It's No Longer Mine to Hold (*Gentle Release*)

Closing Letter to Myself

Your Quotes

About the Author

Thank You for Reading

Introduction

This is not a story about being broken.

This is a story about surviving the breaking.
About waking up inside a life you never chose, and finding a way to choose yourself anyway.

For a long time, I thought survival was the end of the story.
I thought breathing was enough.
I thought less pain meant happiness.
I thought staying silent meant staying safe.

But healing — real healing — showed me that survival is only the beginning.

This book is a map of that journey.
From the first quiet days of endurance,
through the slow, painful awakenings,
through the grief of everything I lost,
into the fierce reclaiming of who I always was underneath it all.

Every stage in these pages is a version of myself I had to live to reach the next one.
None of them were wrong.
None of them were wasted.
They were all necessary steps in finding my way back to me.

I wrote this because I know I'm not the only one.

Maybe you, too, have lived a life that asked you to be smaller than you were born to be.
Maybe you have learned to survive on scraps when you deserved a feast.
Maybe you have spent too long apologizing for your own hope.

If you have — this is for you.

You are not broken.
You are not weak.
You are not too late.

You are surviving, you are dreaming, you are rising.

And you are allowed — always — to want more.

This is not a story about being broken.
This is a story about becoming whole.

Welcome.

Breathing Because I Had To (*Silent Survival*)

"Some days, survival is its own quiet kind of victory."

There wasn't a moment when I decided to survive.
There wasn't a war cry or a grand declaration.
There was just morning after morning where I woke up still breathing,
because stopping didn't seem like an option
even if it didn't feel like a victory either.

In that town, survival wasn't hope.
It wasn't even life.
It was a slow, gray drifting —
a stubborn, exhausted carrying of a weight I didn't remember picking up.

They broke me carefully.
Not with cruelty I could name,
but with silences I didn't know how to argue against,
with expectations I could never quite meet,
with small humiliations dressed up as help.

And after a while, you stop questioning it.
You stop fighting.
You lower your head and you carry the weight
because it's easier than believing there might be another way.
There's no dream in survival.
There's no joy in it.
There's just the quiet knowledge that leaving hurts, but staying hurts less
loudly.

I learned how to make myself small enough to fit inside the space they
allowed me.
I learned how to call that safety.
I learned how to call that kindness.

And when I lay awake at night, staring into the ceiling,
I told myself that this was what healing must look like —
because I was no longer screaming.

I wasn't happy.
I wasn't free.
But I wasn't breaking anymore, and in a life made of bruises,
even that felt like something worth clinging to.

So I kept breathing.

Not because I was brave.

Not because I believed in better.
But because I didn't know how to stop.

And for a long time,
that was enough.

— • —

The Lie I Lived (*Disillusionment*)

"The truth always starts small — a crack, a whisper, a knowing you can't unhear."

For a long time, I believed the story they told me.
That I was broken.
That I was saved.
That I owed my survival to the hands that had first buried me.

It's a beautiful lie, when you're too tired to question it.
It sounds almost like kindness.

They pull you out of the pit they pushed you into
and tell you it was a rescue.
They offer you the scraps they left behind
and call it a feast.

And because you're starved — for love, for safety, for any sliver of peace —
you believe them.
You clutch the scraps with trembling hands and say "thank you."
You call their cruelty mercy because you don't remember what real mercy
feels like anymore.

But lies rot over time.

And no matter how tightly you close your eyes,
there comes a day when the stench of it becomes too strong to ignore.

One day, I realized the helping hands held the same fingerprints as the
ones that hurt me.
One day, I realized that survival shouldn't feel like shame.
That healing shouldn't come with a price tag.
That kindness shouldn't come with a chain.

It didn't happen in a single moment.
It wasn't a lightning strike.

It was a slow, sickening knowing
that crept in around the edges,
until the whole bright picture they painted started to peel and fade,
and underneath, all I saw was rot.

The people who said they loved me
loved me better when I was small.
They loved me better when I was grateful.
They loved me better when I was easier to hold down.

The lie I lived was simple:
that surviving their world meant belonging in it.
That pain was the price of acceptance.
That shrinking was safety.

But the truth was simpler still:

I never truly belonged there.
And somewhere deep inside, under all the bruises and silence,
a small, stubborn voice was starting to remember that.

— • —

The Girl I Forgot (*Grieving the Old Self*)
"There are parts of me I had to lose before I learned how much they mattered."

Before the bruises,
before the bargaining,
before the long slow lessons in silence —
there was a girl who didn't know how to be small.

She laughed too loudly.
She dreamed without shrinking.
She loved with both hands open, never thinking it could cost her.

She didn't know the world could close around her like a fist.
She didn't know the price they would demand for her light.
She didn't know that trusting the wrong hands
could teach you to doubt your own.

And for a long time, after the breaking started,
I forgot her.

I forgot what it felt like to want boldly.
I forgot what it felt like to speak without fear.
I forgot what it felt like to move through the world
without waiting for punishment.

I called that forgetting survival.
I called that forgetting maturity.
I called that forgetting strength.

But it wasn't.

It was grief.
It was mourning.
It was laying down the brightest parts of myself
just to fit into a world too small for the girl I had been.

And even now, after all the surviving and the clawing back,
sometimes I wonder about her.
The girl I forgot.

What would she have built
if no one had taught her to live so quietly?

What would she have dreamed
if no one had taught her to be so careful?

What would she have become
if no one had taught her that wanting was dangerous?

I grieve her not because she is gone —
but because I left her behind for so long without even saying goodbye.

And somewhere inside me,
she is still waiting.
Still daring to laugh.
Still daring to dream.

And one day, I will meet her again.
I will take her hand.
I will tell her: "I'm sorry I left you. I didn't know better. I do now."

And together,
we will begin again.

— • —

Living on Leftovers (*Bittersweet Survival*)

"Not every victory tastes sweet. Some just taste like breathing."

There's a kind of survival that feels almost like happiness. Almost.

You tell yourself the ache in your chest is normal.
You tell yourself the hollow spaces inside you are just what life feels like after growing up.
You tell yourself this is better — and technically, you're not wrong.

There are no more breakdowns behind locked doors.
There are no more nights spent choking on your own silence.
You can laugh again, sometimes.
You can breathe without flinching, most days.

But somewhere deep inside, you know.

You know you're living on leftovers.
You know you're building a life out of scraps —
pieces of dreams you were once too scared to fully claim,
bits of hope you salvaged after the fire.

You survived, yes.
But survival is not the same as living.

And gratitude tastes different when you realize you were fed only after being starved.
Kindness looks different when you realize it came from the same hands that first took everything away.

I smiled.
I said thank you.
I played the part of the one who was saved.
Because it was easier than asking the dangerous question:
"Is this all there is?"

For a long time, it was enough.
Enough to not hurt.
Enough to not fear.
Enough to not want.

But survival without wanting is not a life.
It's an echo of one.

And the hollow in my chest grew louder with every silent, smiling day.

Until one day,
even the leftovers weren't enough anymore.

— • —

I Was Never Theirs (*Defiance and Reclaiming*)

"The fire they thought they extinguished was only sleeping."

They told the story like they saved me.
Like they reached down into the wreckage and pulled me back to life.

They tell it still, sometimes.
Whispered between themselves like a hymn of their own goodness.
A way to polish the guilt off their hands without ever admitting
they were the ones who set the fire first.

But here's what they'll never say:

I survived despite them.
Not because of them.

I kept breathing when they made it easier to stop.
I kept hoping when they tried to teach me not to.
I kept wanting, even in the smallest, most secret corners of myself,
when they told me wanting was dangerous.

They never saved me.
They broke me, and when the breaking made me quiet enough to be convenient,
they called it healing.

But my spirit never belonged to them.
Not for one second.

They mistook my survival for surrender.
They mistook my silence for gratitude.

They thought they had written the ending of my story —
me, small and tame, forever thankful for being allowed to stay.

But they never owned me.
Not then.
Not now.

The bruises faded.

The silence broke.
The girl they buried learned to dig herself free.

And when I rose —
when I stood, not with permission but with purpose —
I didn't rise to thank them.

I rose to reclaim what they thought they'd stolen for good.

My voice.
My hunger.
My dreams.
My fury.

Every part of me they tried to break apart
has come back together sharper, stronger, unstoppable.

I was never theirs.

I am mine.

I always have been.

— • —

You Did What You Had To (*Compassion for the Past Self*)

"Forgiveness starts when you stop punishing yourself for doing what you had to do to survive."

I used to hate the version of me who stayed.

The girl who smiled when she wanted to scream.
The girl who said "thank you" for bruises disguised as blessings.
The girl who learned how to be small, because no one ever taught her she could be anything else.

I wanted to shake her.
I wanted to tear the silence from her throat.
I wanted to scream at her: Run. Fight. Don't you see what they're doing to you?

But I see it differently now.

She stayed because she had to.
She stayed because survival isn't always a battle you can win by force.
Sometimes, survival is endurance.
Sometimes, survival is making yourself small enough to slip through the cracks.
Sometimes, survival is calling the cage a home
because hope hurts too much.

She wasn't weak.
She was surviving the only way she knew how.

And maybe she couldn't fight yet.
Maybe she couldn't leave yet.
Maybe she couldn't even imagine a world outside the one she was trapped in.

But she kept breathing.

She carried the pieces of me forward, even when she didn't know what they were for.
She kept the smallest flame alive — hidden, shielded, stubborn —

so that when the time finally came,
there would still be something left to save.

I owe her everything.

Not shame.
Not anger.

Gratitude.

Because she did what she had to do to get me here.

And now that I know better,
now that I can choose differently,
I will carry her forward too.

Not as a failure.
Not as a wound.
But as a survivor.

A part of me worth loving,
exactly as she was.

— • —

Learning to Want Again (*Dreaming Again*)

"Wanting again is a revolution of the soul."

For a long time, I thought wanting was dangerous.
Wanting meant reaching too far.
Wanting meant exposing yourself to disappointment, to punishment, to pain.
Wanting meant asking for too much.

And so, I stopped.

I stopped dreaming.
I stopped asking.
I stopped hoping.

I told myself I was safer without the ache of possibility.
I told myself I was stronger without the hunger.

But survival without wanting is hollow.
Living without dreaming is just breathing in and out, waiting for the day to end.

And then - slowly, almost without my permission -
the wanting came back.

It started small.

A dream I didn't dare say out loud.
A laugh that escaped too freely.
A longing that stirred in my chest when I thought of something more than just surviving.

At first, I was afraid of it.
I tried to push it down.
I tried to remind myself that safety lived in smallness.

But hope has a stubborn heartbeat.

It kept tapping against my ribs, gentle but relentless,
until I could no longer pretend I didn't hear it.

And when I finally listened,
I realized something powerful:

Wanting is not weakness.
Hoping is not danger.
Dreaming is not foolishness.

Wanting is how we tell the world: I am still alive.

Dreaming is how we declare: I believe there can be more.

So I let myself dream again.
Clumsily.
Tenderly.
Bravely.

I dared to want joy, not just survival.
I dared to want love that didn't ask me to shrink.
I dared to want a life built from abundance, not leftovers.

And every small dream I claimed was an act of rebellion.
Every hope I held was a quiet revolution against everything they taught me.

I am learning, every day,
that I deserve to want.
That I deserve to build a life beyond survival.

And wanting, for the first time in a long time,
feels like coming home.

— • —

It's No Longer Mine to Hold (*Gentle Release*)
"Healing is not forgetting. Healing is no longer needing to hold it so tightly."

There was a time I thought healing would feel like triumph.
A battle won, a flag planted on some high mountain.
Loud. Victorious. Unmistakable.

But it didn't happen like that.

It happened slowly.
Quietly.
Almost without ceremony.

It happened when I realized
I didn't have to keep carrying the weight of what they did to me.
I didn't have to keep stitching their damage into the seams of my story.
I didn't have to hold the anger like armor.
I didn't have to hold the sadness like proof.

None of it was mine to carry anymore.

It shaped me, yes.
It taught me, yes.
It carved lines into my life I will never fully erase.

But it does not define me.
It does not own me.
It does not get to write the ending.

I am more than the bruises.
More than the battles.
More than the survival.

I am the choosing.
I am the dreaming.
I am the rising.

I don't have to hold their mistakes.
I don't have to hold the version of me who believed them.
I don't even have to hold the pain they left behind.

I can set it all down.
Gently.
Finally.
Without apology.

It does not mean it didn't happen.
It does not mean it didn't hurt.
It simply means it does not belong to me anymore.

I belong to myself now.
Completely.
Quietly.
Utterly free.

— • —

Closing Letter to Myself

Dear Me,

You made it.

You survived nights that tried to silence you,
days that pressed you smaller and smaller until you forgot the shape of yourself.
You survived not because it was easy,
not because it was fair,
but because some part of you - the fiercest, most stubborn part - refused to disappear.

I know how tired you were.
I know how lonely it felt, carrying hope like a secret you weren't allowed to have.
I know there were days you thought surviving was all you would ever be allowed.

But you didn't stay there.
You didn't settle.

You chose to want again.
You chose to dream again.
You chose to believe there was a life beyond the edges of survival.

And every choice you made,
every tear you cried,
every small rebellion of hope in the darkness -
it brought you here.

Here, where you can breathe without asking permission.
Here, where you can laugh without shrinking.
Here, where you can build without fear.
Here, where you belong to no one but yourself.

There is no shame in the girl who stayed too long.
There is no shame in the girl who forgot how to dream.
There is no shame in the girl who called survival enough,

because she was doing the best she could with what she knew.

Honor her.
Thank her.
But know this:
You are no longer living her story.

You are writing something new now.
And it is bigger, braver, and more beautiful than anything they ever taught you to expect.

You are whole.
You are free.
You are enough - not because you survived them,
but because you were always enough.

Even when you couldn't see it yet.

I am proud of you.
I am proud of every version of you.

And I will carry you forward with love,
always.

- Me

Your Quotes

This book was never meant to be read passively.
It was meant to be felt.
It was meant to be lived through.

Here is your space —
to gather the words that stayed with you,
the lines that shook something loose,
the truths that found you exactly where you are.

Fill this page with whatever resonated.
Your favorite quotes.
Your favorite feelings.
Your survival written back to yourself.

There are no wrong choices.
This is your story too.

Favorite Lines:

_____

_____

_____

_____

_____

_____

_____

_____

"The words you hold onto are the ones already holding onto you."

About the Author

Flora Martin writes because some stories don't disappear when the hurting ends — they ask to be carried forward, honored, and healed.

She believes that survival is sacred.
That grief deserves its voice.
That dreaming after pain is an act of wild, breathtaking courage.

This book is not just her story.
It is a map for anyone who has forgotten, and remembered, and survived all over again.

In every word, she offers this truth:
you were always enough — even when you could not see it yet.

Thank You for Reading

Thank you for walking these pages with me.
For carrying the heavy moments, the soft ones, and everything in between.

If you found parts of yourself inside these words —
the dreaming parts, the grieving parts, the surviving parts —
know that you are seen.

Know that you are not alone.

The story you are living now is still yours to shape.
It is still yours to claim.
It is still yours to rise from.

You are already enough.

You always have been.

Thank you for being here.

Made in the USA
Coppell, TX
22 January 2026

66422200R00021